Sampler Spree

100+ Fresh & Fun Quilt Blocks

Susan Ache

Martingale®
Create with Confidence

Sampler Spree: 100+ Fresh & Fun Quilt Blocks
© 2021 by Susan Ache

Martingale®
18939 120th Ave. NE, Ste. 101
Bothell, WA 98011-9511 USA
ShopMartingale.com

Printed in Hong Kong
26 25 24 23 22 21   8 7 6 5 4 3 2 1

Library of Congress Cataloging-in-Publication Data is available upon request.

ISBN: 978-1-68356-122-4

MISSION STATEMENT

We empower makers who use fabric and yarn to make life more enjoyable.

CREDITS

PUBLISHER AND
CHIEF VISIONARY OFFICER
Jennifer Erbe Keltner

CONTENT DIRECTOR
Karen Costello Soltys

MANAGING EDITOR
Tina Cook

ACQUISITIONS AND
DEVELOPMENT EDITOR
Laurie Baker

TECHNICAL EDITOR
Nancy Mahoney

COPY EDITOR
Melissa Bryan

DESIGN MANAGER
Adrienne Smitke

PRODUCTION MANAGER
Regina Girard

LOCATION PHOTOGRAPHER
Adam Albright

STUDIO PHOTOGRAPHER
Brent Kane

ILLUSTRATOR
Sandy Loi

SPECIAL THANKS
Photography for this book was taken at the home of Libby Warnken in Ankeny, Iowa.

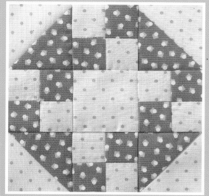

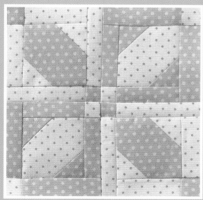

Table of Contents

Let's Get Scrappy!

It's true confession time: I love making quilt blocks. I love picking fabrics, stitching sample blocks, and in short, playing in my fabric scraps. It's absolutely my favorite part of quilting. Of course, I love displaying and using my finished quilts. But more than that, I'm a process person who gets excited about playing with fabric and piecing quilt blocks!

When the opportunity came to write a quilt-block book, do you know what I did first? I went to my bin of orphan blocks—ones I had pieced to see how they'd look, try a new technique or ruler, or test a new color combination. I save these blocks because you never know when you might need them. Turns out, they came in quite handy for this book!

I didn't use all of my orphan blocks as they were, but I revisited them and remade some in new colorways. I modified others to make them easier to piece. And then I designed some new blocks specifically for this book. I had a grand time playing with fabrics, planning color schemes, and thinking about how to sash the blocks. My hope is that you'll have just as much fun, whether you make a quilt using 100 different blocks, mix and match just a few blocks for a smaller quilt, or pick a favorite block and repeat it across a quilt top.

No matter which blocks capture your attention, be sure to look through all the pages because sprinkled throughout the book are some of my favorite tips. You'll read about planning color schemes, using your scraps (by all means, start with your scrap bin—you already know you love those fabrics!), and looking at blocks in a whole new way with the help of your smartphone.

So what are you waiting for? Let's get scrappy and make some quilts! Be sure to post pictures on social media using the tag #SamplerSpree, so we can all share in the excitement.

Happy stitching,
Susan

How to Use This Book

The Give and Take quilt (page 8) contains 100 patchwork blocks. The individual blocks are numbered and the quilt assembly diagram on page 12 shows where I placed each block number in my layout, should you want to do the same. I've also included six extra blocks in case you wish to substitute a block in the quilt layout, or if you'd just like more blocks to make your own quilt designs! Each block measures 6" square (finished). Following are some handy notes about the cutting instructions as well as the shortcut techniques I've used in piecing the blocks.

Cutting Icons

Cutting instructions for the blocks are simplified for convenience, with individual pieces (squares, triangles, and rectangles) shown as symbols. The following cutting symbols are used throughout the block patterns to indicate the shapes to cut:

☐ Cut squares in the specified dimensions.

▭ Cut rectangles in the specified dimensions.

◻ A square with a diagonal line through it means to cut the square in half diagonally to make two triangles with the bias along the long edge.

⊠ A square with two crossed lines means to cut the square into quarters diagonally to make four triangles with the bias along the short edges.

▱ A rectangle with a diagonal line through it means to cut the rectangle in half diagonally. Make sure to place the rectangle right side up before cutting and cut in the direction shown in the block photo.

Half-Square-Triangle Units

Layer squares of two different fabrics right sides together. Draw a diagonal line from corner to corner on the wrong side of the lighter square. Stitch ¼" from both sides of the drawn line. Cut the squares apart on the drawn line to make two matching half-square-triangle (HST) units. Press the seam allowances toward the darker fabric.

Flying-Geese Units

Flying geese are made from a rectangle and two squares. Draw a diagonal line from corner to corner on the wrong side of each square. Place a marked square on one end of the rectangle, right sides together with the marked line angled as shown below. Stitch on the marked line. Trim ¼" from the stitched line. Flip the triangle up and press the seam allowances toward the corner. Repeat on the opposite end of the rectangle, positioning the diagonal line in the opposite direction as shown.

 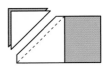

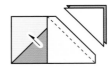 

Stitch-and-Flip Corners

Use the stitch-and-flip method to add a triangle to a corner without actually using a triangle! Draw a diagonal line on the wrong side of the designated square, which is smaller than the piece it will be stitched to. Place the square on a corner of the larger square, rectangle, or pieced unit, right sides together. Angle the line as shown. Stitch on the line. Trim ¼" from the stitched line, flip the triangle up, and press the seam allowances toward the corner.

Rectangle-to-Rectangle Units

I love when I can avoid using a template, and that's just what this technique does. On the wrong side of a rectangle, align the 45° line of a square ruler with a long edge of the rectangle and draw a diagonal line. Note that to join three rectangles, you need to draw the line on the second rectangle in the opposite direction from the first one. Layer a marked rectangle on top of the base rectangle, lining up the corners. Stitch on the line. Trim ¼" from the stitched line. Open the rectangles and press the seam allowances toward the darker fabric.

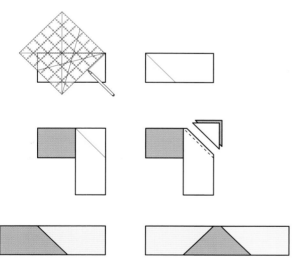

Two rectangles sewn together   Three rectangles sewn together

Templates

Even though I'm a fan of avoiding templates when I can, you'll need to make templates for a few of the blocks. To make a template, trace the pattern onto template plastic. Use utility scissors to cut out the template *exactly* on the drawn lines. Always place the right side of the template *face up* on the right side of the fabric. Some blocks require a reverse image, in which case you simply need to flip the template over so that the right side of the template is *face down* on the right side of the fabric.

Rulers

For a couple of the blocks that involve templates, you may wish to use a specialty ruler for cutting instead. Refer to the pattern provided with the block instructions to determine which line on the ruler to align with the edge of the fabric or strip set. If you are unfamiliar with a ruler, be sure to read the manufacturer's instructions. Here are the rulers I used:

Block 6: Bloc Loc Kite in a Square 3" x 3" ruler set.

Block 37: Bloc Loc Triangle in a Square 2" × 2" ruler set or Tri-Recs Tools by Darlene Zimmerman and Joy Hoffman to cut the large and small triangles.

Block 49: Companion Angle ruler by Darlene Zimmerman. Align the 3½" line with the outer edges of the strip set.

Block 60: Easy Angle ruler by Sharon Hultgren. Align the bottom of the ruler with the outer edges of the strip set.

So Many Tips!

In addition to all the blocks and the quilt pattern, you'll also find many tips sprinkled throughout this book. They are not meant to relate specifically to any one block, but rather they're tips for rotary cutting, piecing patchwork, pressing for accuracy, and even storing blocks and pieces. So be sure to read all the tips, even if they're not on the page of block instructions you're following at the moment!

Give and Take

Scrappy is the name of the game for *Give and Take*, a quilt that's fun to make and a joy to behold. Notice how the sashing arrangement makes the layout seem to push and pull as your eye moves around the quilt. Here's your chance to showcase all those bits and pieces of treasured fabrics in a quilt that vibrates with excitement!

Finished quilt: 83½" × 83½" | Finished block: 13" × 13"

Materials

Yardage is based on 42"-wide fabric.

1 yard *total* of assorted cream prints for large blocks

3 yards *total* of assorted light scraps for blocks

3⅞ yards *total* of assorted medium and dark scraps (referred to collectively as "dark") for blocks

1¼ yards of white solid for sashing

2⅜ yards of peach solid for sashing and binding

7¾ yards of fabric for backing

92" × 92" piece of batting

Cutting and Piecing the Blocks

Using the assorted scraps, refer to pages 13–75 to make 100 blocks. The featured quilt shown on page 11 uses one each of blocks 1–100, but block designs 101–106 are provided for variety in case you wish to make any substitutions. Each block should measure 6½" square, including seam allowances. Follow the instructions below to cut pieces for the rest of the quilt. All measurements include ¼" seam allowances.

From the assorted cream prints, cut a *total* of:
25 sets of 4 matching rectangles, 1½" × 6½"

From the assorted dark scraps, cut a *total* of:
25 squares, 1½" × 1½"

From the white solid, cut:
3 strips, 13½" × 42"; crosscut into 60 strips, 2" × 13½"

From the peach solid, cut:
3 strips, 13½" × 42"; crosscut into 60 strips, 2" × 13½"
4 strips, 3½" × 42"; crosscut into 36 squares, 3½" × 3½"
9 strips, 2¼" × 42"

Assembling the Quilt Top

Press all seam allowances as indicated by the arrows.

1. Lay out four blocks, four matching cream rectangles, and one dark 1½" square in three rows. Sew the pieces into rows. Join the rows to make a large block. Make 25 large blocks measuring 13½" square, including seam allowances.

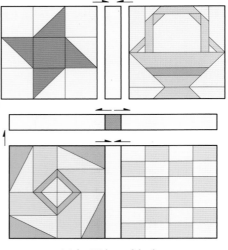

Make 25 large blocks,
13½" × 13½".

2. Join the white and peach 2" × 13½" strips to make 60 sashing strips measuring 3½" × 13½", including seam allowances.

Make 60 strips,
3½" × 13½".

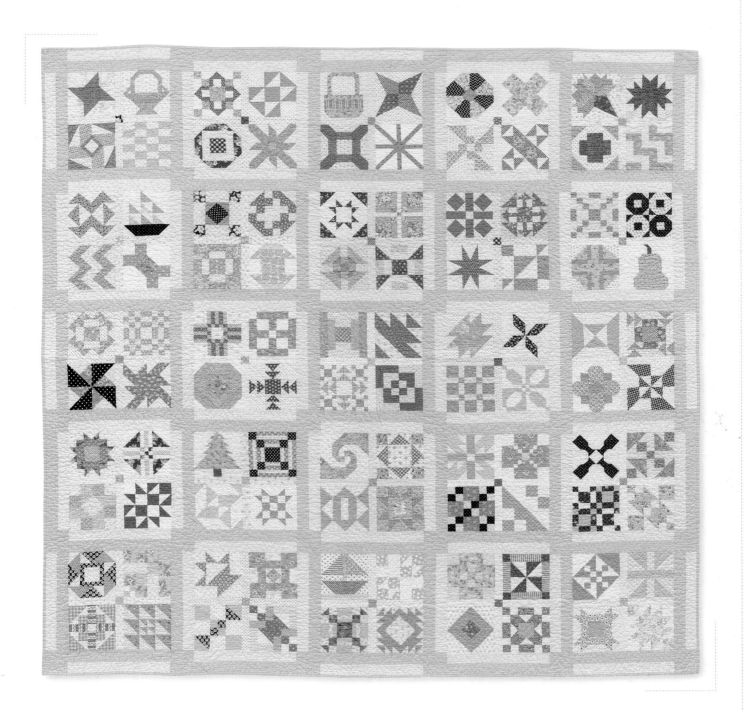

3. Lay out the large blocks, sashing strips, and peach squares in 11 rows as shown in the quilt assembly diagram below. Sew the pieces into rows. Join the rows to complete the quilt top, which should measure 83½" square.

Finishing the Quilt

For more details on any finishing steps, visit ShopMartingale.com/HowtoQuilt for free downloadable information.

1. Layer the quilt top with batting and backing; baste the layers together.

2. Quilt by hand or machine. The quilt shown is machine quilted with an allover rose motif.

3. Use the peach 2¼"-wide strips to make binding, and then attach the binding to the quilt.

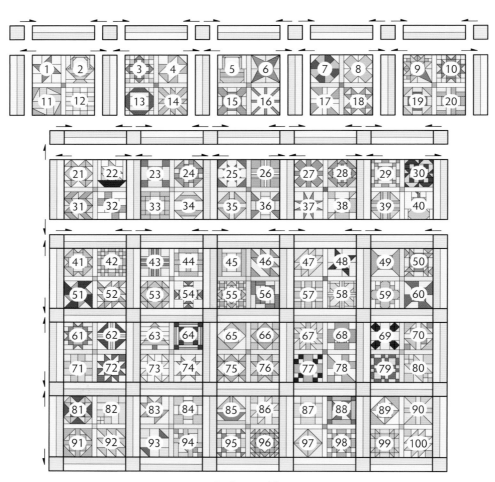

Quilt assembly

The Blocks

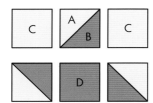 **01** *Friendship Star*

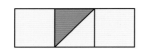

Using A/B, make 2½" HST units (page 6).

Light
A: 2 ☐ 2⅞" × 2⅞"
C: 4 ☐ 2½" × 2½"

Dark
B: 2 ☐ 2⅞" × 2⅞"
D: 1 ☐ 2½" × 2½"

Susan's Scrappy Secrets

* **If I've never made a particular block before,** I always sew a test block. And because I like to make a lot of sampler quilts, I make test blocks using solids so that I will have extra fillers for future samplers.

* **Test blocks are important.** They are a way to know if you want to keep repeating the same block in one quilt (or is once enough?!). They also help you work out where there may be a shortcut in the process.

* **When making extra half-square-triangle or flying-geese units** from block leftovers, I don't bother trimming them. Later on, when I want to use them, I can trim them to whatever size I need for my new project.

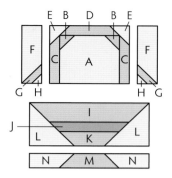

Using B, E, G, H, and L, make stitch-and-flip corners (page 7). Using M and N, make rectangle-to-rectangle units (page 7).

Light

A: 1 ▭ 3" × 3½"
E: 2 ▭ 1½" × 1½"
F: 2 ▭ 1½" × 3½"
H: 2 ▭ 1" × 1"
L: 2 ▭ 2¾" × 2¾"
N: 2 ▭ 1¼" × 2¾"

Medium

B: 2 ▭ 1¼" × 1¼"
C: 2 ▭ 1" × 3"
D: 1 ▭ 1" × 4½"
G: 2 ▭ 1½" × 1½"
I: 1 ▭ 1½" × 6½"
K: 1 ▭ 1¼" × 6½"
M: 1 ▭ 1¼" × 3½"

Dark

J: 1 ▭ 1" × 6½"

✷ **I always cut setting triangles oversized when making an on-point quilt.** Doing so makes it so much easier to trim them down to the exact seam allowance, rather than trying to fudge it.

✷ **Once a year I take out my stacks of colors from my stash** (I organize all fabrics by color), and reevaluate whether I've outgrown any of the prints and no longer love them. I pass those fabrics on to someone who will give them new life.

✷ **I begin every single quilt working from my scrap bin first.** For a scrappy quilt to look super scrappy, it's more fun to actually play with scraps first and fill in with cut yardage as you go.

03 Susan's Chain

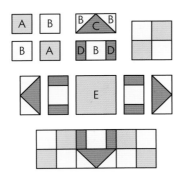

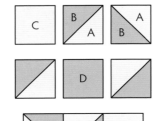

Using B/C, make 1½" × 2½" flying-geese units (page 6).

Medium
A: 8 ☐ 1½" × 1½"
E: 1 ☐ 2½" × 2½"

Light
B: 20 ☐ 1½" × 1½"

Dark
C: 4 ☐ 1½" × 2½"
D: 8 ☐ 1" × 1½"

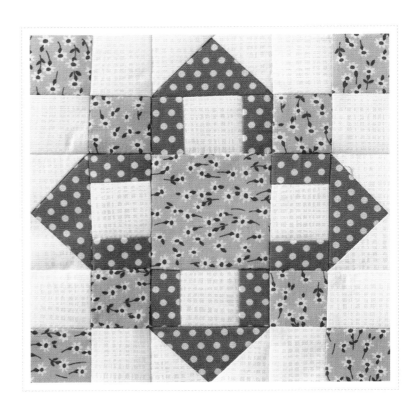

04 Split Nine Patch

Using A/B, make 2½" HST units (page 6).

Light
A: 3 ☐ 2⅞" × 2⅞"
C: 2 ☐ 2½" × 2½"

Dark
B: 3 ☐ 2⅞" × 2⅞"
D: 1 ☐ 2½" × 2½"

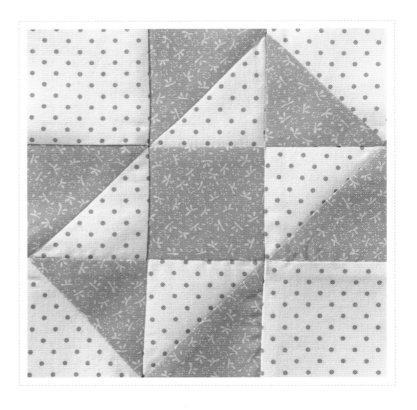

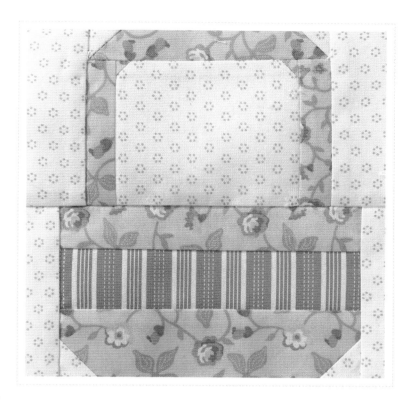

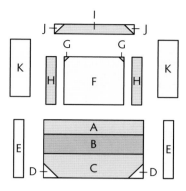

05 Easter Basket

Using D, G, and J, make stitch-and-flip corners (page 7).

Mediums

A: 1 ▭ 1¼" × 5½"

C: 1 ▭ 1¾" × 5½"

G: 2 ▭ ¾" × ¾"

H: 2 ▭ 1" × 3"

I: 1 ▭ 1" × 4½"

Dark

B: 1 ▭ 1½" × 5½"

Light

D: 2 ▭ 1¼" × 1¼"

E: 2 ▭ 1" × 3½"

F: 1 ▭ 3" × 3½"

J: 2 ▭ 1" × 1"

K: 2 ▭ 1½" × 3½"

Susan's Scrappy Secrets

★ **When it comes to fabric in a scrappy quilt,** I follow the rule of odd numbers. I want any given fabric to show up one, three, or five times, rather than twice.

★ **If I have a fabric I really love but it doesn't seem to work well with other fabrics in my plan,** I play around with the fabric placement to make it work. That way I always know I have a piece of something I really love in the quilt.

★ **I'm not a perfectionist,** but I do try my best to not let a mistake that's easily correctable pass me by. There's always enough time to resew a seam that doesn't match up or correct a point that's been chopped off.

06 *Kites*

Use the patterns on page 77 to make templates (page 7). (See "Rulers" on page 7 to cut the units using a ruler.)

Darks

A: 2 of template A

C: 2 of template A

Lights

B: 2 and 2 reversed of template B

D: 2 and 2 reversed of template B

 07 *Fan Blades*

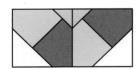

Using A/B, make 3½" HST units (page 6). Using C and D, make stitch-and-flip corners (page 7).

Medium 1

A: 2 ☐ 3⅞" × 3⅞"

Darks

B: 2 ☐ 3⅞" × 3⅞"

Medium 2

C: 4 ☐ 1½" × 1½"

Light

D: 4 ☐ 2½" × 2½"

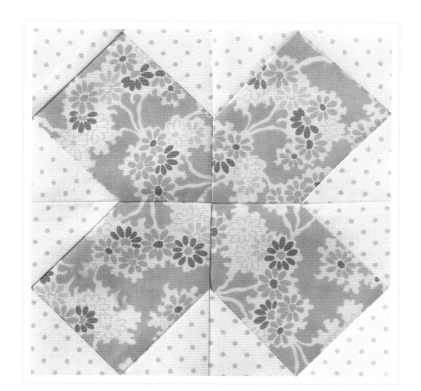

08 Broken Sash

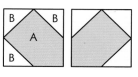

Using B, make stitch-and-flip corners (page 7).

Dark
A: 4 ☐ 3½" × 3½"

Light
B: 12 ☐ 2" × 2"

Susan's Scrappy Secrets

* **When making a two-color quilt,** I use lots of different shades of that color to give it depth. Two color doesn't have to mean just two fabrics!

* **For a vintage feel,** mix whites and creams together in the background.

* **When I'm sewing a lot of the exact same parts for blocks,** I break them down into groups or batches. It elevates my sense of accomplishment!

* **Set aside time in January** to actually try out all of the new tools you've purchased on a whim during the year but actually haven't used. I make it a resolution to see how I can make the best use of each tool or technique moving forward.

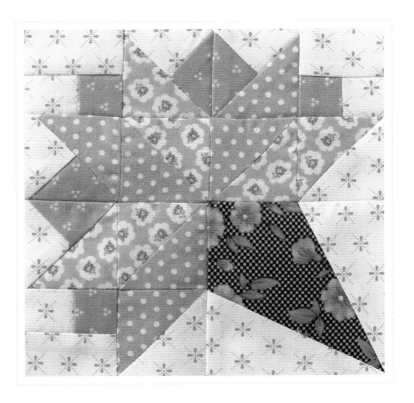

Use the patterns on page 77 to make templates (page 7). Using J/K, J/L, and K/L, make 2" HST units (page 6; 1 of each unit is extra).

Dark

A: 1 of template A

Light

B: 1 and 1 reversed of template B
D: 3 ☐ 1¼" × 1¼"
E: 3 ▭ 1¼" × 2"
F: 1 ⊠ 2¾" × 2¾"
K: 2 ☐ 2⅜" × 2⅜"

Medium 1

C: 3 ☐ 1¼" × 1¼"
G: 1 ⊠ 2¾" × 2¾"

Medium 2

I: 1 ☑ 2⅜" × 2⅜"
L: 3 ☐ 2⅜" × 2⅜"

Medium 3

H: 1 ☑ 2⅜" × 2⅜"
J: 3 ☐ 2⅜" × 2⅜"

Susan's Scrappy Secrets

★ **Check our technique videos on YouTube** or on quilt designers Instagram or Facebook pages. If a technique is new to you or seems difficult or different from what you're used to, it's refreshing to get different perspectives on it.

★ **Do you like to sew from a kit?** Well, I make my own kits from my stash. But rather than store bundles or bins full of kits, I take a photo of my homemade kits and keep the photos stored in a separate album on my phone so I can just pull the fabric when I'm ready to make that project.

10 Squash Blossom

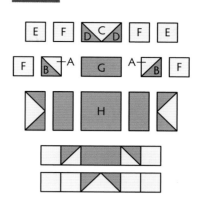

Using A/B, make 1½" HST units (page 6).
Using C/D, make 1½" × 2½" flying-geese units (page 6).

Light
A: 2 ☐ 1⅞" × 1⅞"
C: 4 ▭ 1½" × 2½"
F: 8 ☐ 1½" × 1½"

Medium
E: 4 ☐ 1½" × 1½"

Dark
B: 2 ☐ 1⅞" × 1⅞"
D: 8 ☐ 1½" × 1½"
G: 4 ▭ 1½" × 2½"
H: 1 ☐ 2½" × 2½"

✱ **It's very seldom that I cut binding at the same time as I cut the rest of the quilt.** More often than not, when I get the quilt back from the long-arm quilter, I change my mind because another fabric choice looks better.

✱ **Starting each quilt in a tidy workspace** helps me concentrate and doesn't overwhelm me, even though I may have more projects stacked up waiting to be made.

✱ **How do you store Jelly Rolls, Honey Buns, Layer Cakes, and charm packs?** I open them up, unroll them, and put them into my scrap bins, which are all sorted by color.

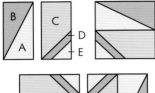

11 Lacy Lattice Work

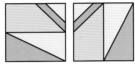

Using A/B, make half-rectangle units; trim to 2" × 3½". Using D and E, make stitch-and-flip corners (page 7).

Light
A: 2 ◿ 2½" × 4½"
E: 4 ☐ 1½" × 1½"

Dark
B: 2 ◿ 2½" × 4½"
D: 4 ☐ 2" × 2"

Medium
C: 4 ▭ 2" × 3½"

12 Patio Pavers

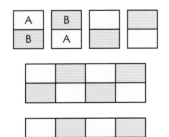

Using A/B, make a strip set; crosscut into 12 segments, 2" × 2½".

Light
A: 1 ▭ 1½" × 26"

Medium
B: 1 ▭ 1½" × 26"

13 The Kitchen Woodbox

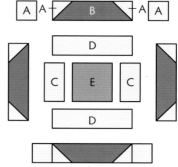

Using A, make stitch-and-flip corners (page 7).

Light
A: 12 □ 1½" × 1½"
C: 2 ▭ 1½" × 2½"
D: 2 ▭ 1½" × 4½"

Darks
B: 4 ▭ 1½" × 4½"
E: 1 □ 2½" × 2½"

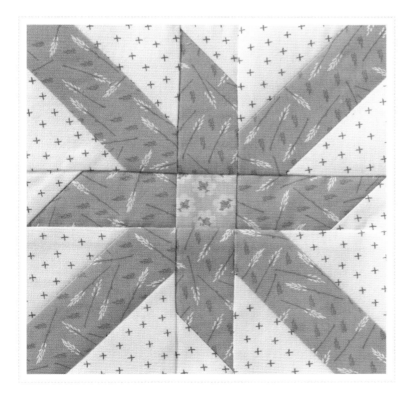

14 Spinster

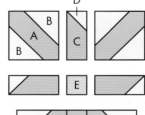

Using B and D, make stitch-and-flip corners (page 7).

Dark
A: 4 □ 3" × 3"
C: 4 ▭ 1½" × 3"

Light
B: 8 □ 2¼" × 2¼"
D: 4 □ 1½" × 1½"

Medium
E: 1 □ 1½" × 1½"

The Blocks

15 Jacksonville Square

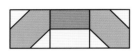

Using B, make stitch-and-flip corners (page 7).

Dark
A: 4 ☐ 2½" × 2½"

Medium
D: 4 ☐ 1½" × 2½"

Light
B: 8 ☐ 1½" × 1½"
C: 4 ☐ 1½" × 2½"
E: 1 ☐ 2½" × 2½"

16 Lattice

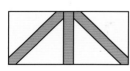

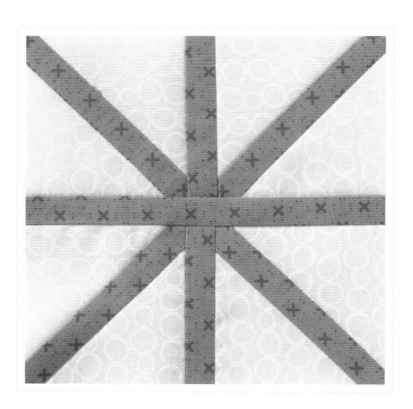

Trim A/B units to 3¼" square.

Light
A: 4 ☐ 4" × 4"

Dark
B: 4 ☐ 1" × 6"
C: 2 ☐ 1" × 3¼"
D: 1 ☐ 1" × 6½"

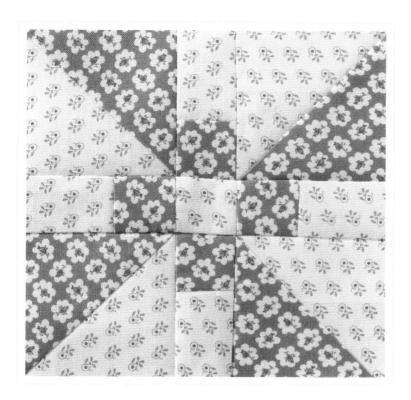

17 Propeller

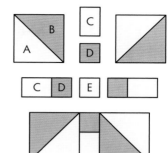

Using A/B, make 3" HST units (page 6).

Light
A: 2 ☐ 3⅜" × 3⅜"
C: 4 ☐ 1½" × 2"
E: 1 ☐ 1½" × 1½"

Dark
B: 2 ☐ 3⅜" × 3⅜"
D: 4 ☐ 1½" × 1½"

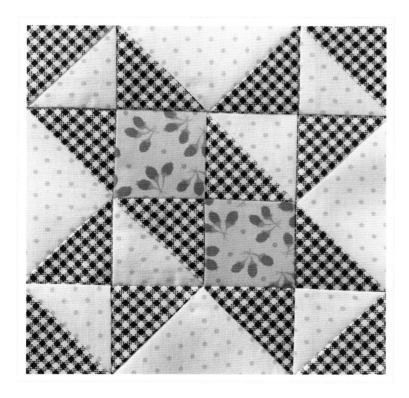

18 Chisholm Trail

Using A/B, make 2" HST units (page 6).
Using D/E, make 2" × 3½" flying-geese units (page 6).

Dark
A: 3 ☐ 2⅜" × 2⅜"
E: 8 ☐ 2" × 2"

Light
B: 3 ☐ 2⅜" × 2⅜"
D: 4 ☐ 2" × 3½"

Medium
C: 2 ☐ 2" × 2"

19 Greek Cross

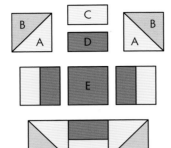

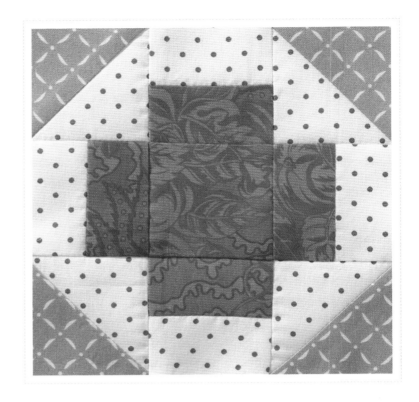

Using A/B, make 2½" HST units (page 6).

Light
A: 2 ☐ 2⅞" × 2⅞"
C: 4 ▭ 1½" × 2½"

Medium
B: 2 ☐ 2⅞" × 2⅞"

Dark
D: 4 ▭ 1½" × 2½"
E: 1 ☐ 2½" × 2½"

20 London Stairs

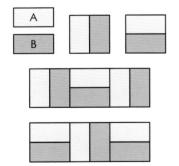

Using A/B, make a strip set; crosscut into 9 segments, 2½" × 2½".

Light
A: 1 ▭ 1½" × 24"

Dark
B: 1 ▭ 1½" × 24"

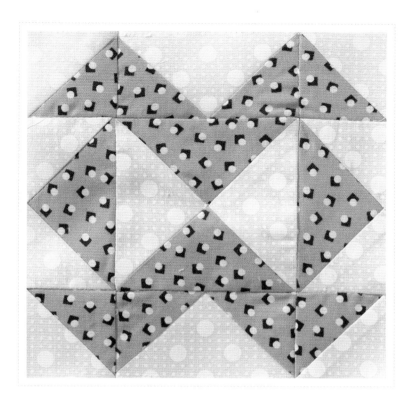

21 Our Editor

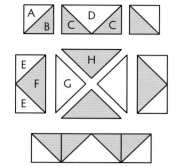

Using A/B, make 2" HST units (page 6).
Using C/D and E/F, make 2" × 3½"
flying-geese units (page 6).

Light	Dark
A: 2 ☐ 2⅜" × 2⅜"	**B:** 2 ☐ 2⅜" × 2⅜"
D: 2 ▭ 2" × 3½"	**C:** 4 ☐ 2" × 2"
E: 4 ☐ 2" × 2"	**F:** 2 ▭ 2" × 3½"
G: 1 ⊠ 4¼" × 4¼"	**H:** 1 ⊠ 4¼" × 4¼"
(2 triangles are extra)	(2 triangles are extra)

Susan's Scrappy Secrets

★ **If I ever need some fresh inspiration** for colors or quilts, I use Google image searches on my computer. The amount of inspiration in photos is vast, and I always click away feeling refreshed.

★ **Want to get real color variety in your scrappy quilts?** Lay out all of the fabrics you want to play with in stacks by color. Make sure the number of fabrics in each color are pretty even. If not, add or subtract so that you have a good color balance.

★ **I don't put away any of the fabric for the project I'm working on until the quilt is complete.** That way I don't have to remember where I put it if I need more, and I know if I have more yardage or just scraps left.

22 Dream Ship

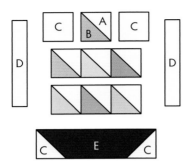

Using A/B, make 2" HST units (page 6; 1 unit is extra). Using C, make stitch-and-flip corners (page 7).

Light
A: 4 ☐ 2⅜" × 2⅜"
C: 4 ☐ 2" × 2"
D: 2 ▭ 1¼" × 5"

Mediums
B: 4 ☐ 2⅜" × 2⅜"

Dark
E: 1 ▭ 2" × 6½"

23 New Album

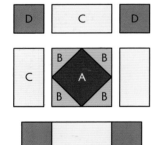

Using B, make stitch-and-flip corners (page 7).

Darks
A: 1 ☐ 3½" × 3½"
D: 4 ☐ 2" × 2"

Medium
B: 4 ☐ 2" × 2"

Light
C: 4 ▭ 2" × 3½"

24 Prairie Queen

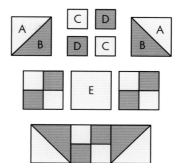

Using A/B, make 2½" HST units (page 6).

Light	Dark
A: 2 ☐ 2⅞" × 2⅞"	**B:** 2 ☐ 2⅞" × 2⅞"
C: 8 ☐ 1½" × 1½"	**D:** 8 ☐ 1½" × 1½"
E: 1 ☐ 2½" × 2½"	

25 Dandy

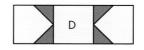

Using A/B, make 2½" HST units (page 6). Using C, make stitch-and-flip corners (page 7).

Light	Dark
A: 2 ☐ 2⅞" × 2⅞"	**B:** 2 ☐ 2⅞" × 2⅞"
D: 5 ☐ 2½" × 2½"	**C:** 8 ☐ 1½" × 1½"

26 Gift Box

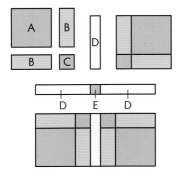

Darks
A: 4 ☐ 2½" × 2½"
B: 8 ☐ 1¼" × 2½"
C: 4 ☐ 1¼" × 1¼"
E: 1 ☐ 1" × 1"

Light
D: 4 ☐ 1" × 3¼"

27 Economy

Using A, make stitch-and-flip corners (page 7).

Light
A: 16 ☐ 1¾" × 1¾"
D: 1 ☐ 1½" × 1½"

Dark
B: 4 ☐ 3" × 3"
C: 4 ☐ 1½" × 3"

28 Prayer Meeting

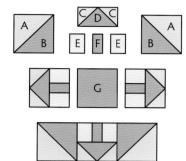

Using A/B, make 2½" HST units (page 6).
Using C/D, make 1½" × 2½" flying-geese units (page 6).

Lights
A: 2 ☐ 2⅞" × 2⅞"
C: 8 ☐ 1½" × 1½"
E: 8 ☐ 1¼" × 1½"

Dark
B: 2 ☐ 2⅞" × 2⅞"
D: 4 ☐ 1½" × 2½"
F: 4 ☐ 1" × 1½"
G: 1 ☐ 2½" × 2½"

29 Grandma's Square

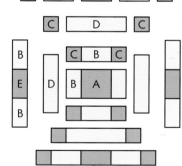

Dark
A: 1 ☐ 2" × 2"
C: 12 ☐ 1¼" × 1¼"
E: 4 ☐ 1¼" × 2"

Light
B: 12 ☐ 1¼" × 2"
D: 4 ☐ 1¼" × 3½"

30 Donuts

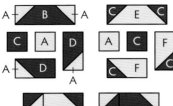

Using A and C, make stitch-and-flip corners (page 7).

Light
A: 12 □ 1½" × 1½"
E: 2 □ 1½" × 3½"
F: 4 □ 1½" × 2½"

Dark
B: 2 □ 1½" × 3½"
C: 12 □ 1½" × 1½"
D: 4 □ 1½" × 2½"

31 Lightning Strikes

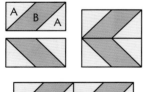

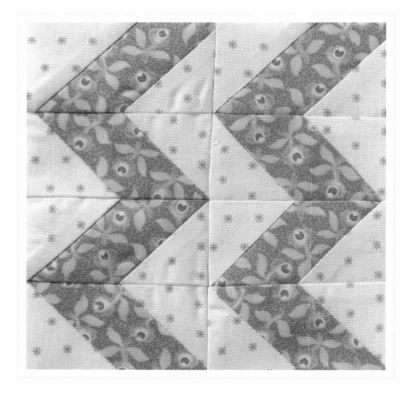

Using A, make stitch-and-flip corners (page 7).

Light
A: 16 □ 2" × 2"

Dark
B: 8 □ 2" × 3½"

32 Mr. Roosevelt's Necktie

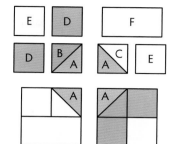

Using A/B and A/C, make 2" HST units (page 6).

Medium
A: 2 ☐ 2⅜" × 2⅜"

Dark
B: 1 ☐ 2⅜" × 2⅜"
D: 4 ☐ 2" × 2"

Light
C: 1 ☐ 2⅜" × 2⅜"
E: 4 ☐ 2" × 2"
F: 2 ▭ 2" × 3½"

33 Antique Tile

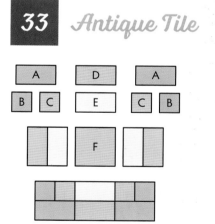

Darks
A: 4 ▭ 1½" × 2½"
B: 4 ☐ 1½" × 1½"
C: 4 ☐ 1½" × 1½"
D: 4 ▭ 1½" × 2½"
F: 1 ☐ 2½" × 2½"

Light
E: 4 ▭ 1½" × 2½"

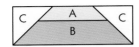 **34** *Buoy*

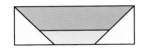

Using C, make stitch-and-flip corners (page 7).

Medium
A: 2 ▭ 1¼" × 6½"

Dark
B: 2 ▭ 1¾" × 6½"
D: 1 ▭ 2½" × 3½"

Light
C: 4 ▭ 2½" × 2½"
E: 2 ▭ 2" × 2½"

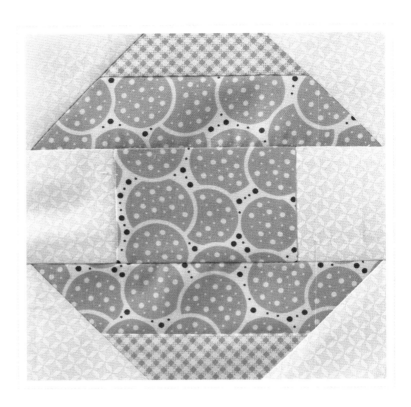

---

35 *Double Shoo Fly*

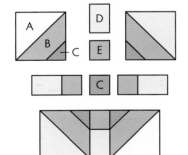

Using A/B, make 3" HST units (page 6).
Using C, make stitch-and-flip corners (page 7).

Light
A: 2 ▭ 3⅜" × 3⅜"
D: 4 ▭ 1½" × 2"

Darks
B: 2 ▭ 3⅜" × 3⅜"
C: 5 ▭ 1½" × 1½"
E: 4 ▭ 1½" × 1½"

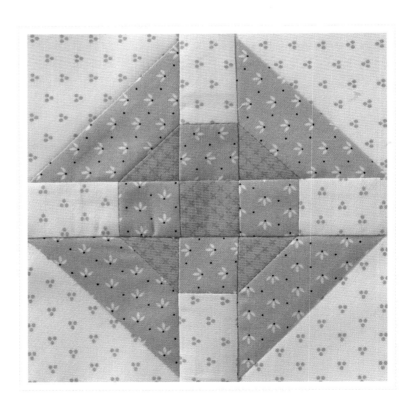

36 Farm Friendliness

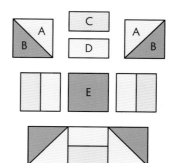

Using A/B, make 2½" HST units (page 6).

Light
A: 2 ☐ 2⅞" × 2⅞"
D: 4 ▭ 1½" × 2½"

Dark
B: 2 ☐ 2⅞" × 2⅞"
E: 1 ☐ 2½" × 2½"

Medium
C: 4 ▭ 1½" × 2½"

37 Sun Rays

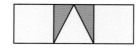

Use the patterns on page 78 to make templates (page 7). (See "Rulers" on page 7 to cut the units using a ruler.) Using A/B, make 2½" units.

Light
A: 4 of template A
C: 4 ☐ 2½" × 2½"

Dark
B: 4 and 4 reversed of template B
D: 1 ☐ 2½" × 2½"

38 *Summer Solstice*

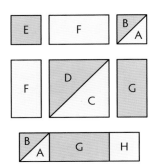

Using A/B, make 2" HST units (page 6).
Using C/D, make 3½" HST units (1 unit is extra).

Light
A: 1 ▢ 2⅜" × 2⅜"
C: 1 ▢ 3⅞" × 3⅞"
F: 2 ▭ 2" × 3½"
H: 1 ▢ 2" × 2"

Dark
B: 1 ▢ 2⅜" × 2⅜"
D: 1 ▢ 3⅞" × 3⅞"
E: 1 ▢ 2" × 2"
G: 2 ▭ 2" × 3½"

39 *Friendship Quilt*

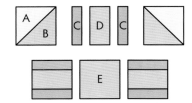

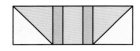

Using A/B, make 2½" HST units (page 6).

Light
A: 2 ▢ 2⅞" × 2⅞"

Dark
C: 8 ▭ 1" × 2½"

Medium
B: 2 ▢ 2⅞" × 2⅞"
D: 4 ▭ 1½" × 2½"
E: 1 ▢ 2½" × 2½"

40 Pear

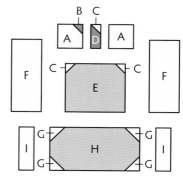

Using B, C, and G, make stitch-and-flip corners (page 7).

Light

A: 2 □ 1¾" × 1¾"

C: 3 □ 1" × 1"

F: 2 □ 2" × 4¼"

G: 4 □ 1¼" × 1¼"

I: 2 □ 1¼" × 2¾"

Dark

B: 1 □ 1" × 1"

D: 1 □ 1" × 1¾"

Medium

E: 1 □ 3" × 3½"

H: 1 □ 2¾" × 5"

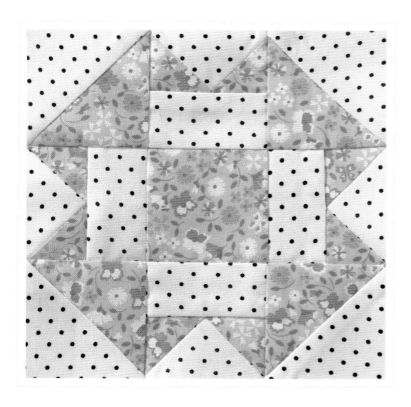

41 Big T

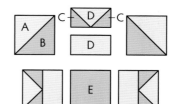

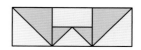

Using A/B, make 2½" HST units (page 6). Using C/D, make 1½" × 2½" flying-geese units (page 6).

Light

A: 2 □ 2⅞" × 2⅞"

D: 8 □ 1½" × 2½"

Dark

B: 2 □ 2⅞" × 2⅞"

C: 8 □ 1½" × 1½"

E: 1 □ 2½" × 2½"

42 *Building Blocks*

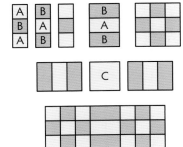

Using A/B/A, make a strip set; crosscut into 8 segments, 1¼" × 2¾". Using B/A/B, make 2 strip sets; crosscut into 4 segments, 2" × 2¾", and 4 segments, 1¼" × 2¾".

Light
A: 4 ▭ 1¼" × 11"
C: 1 ☐ 2" × 2"

Dark
B: 5 ▭ 1¼" × 11"

Susan's Scrappy Secrets

★ **Don't empty your sewing room trash bin** until the project you're working on is finished. I've had to hunt through my trash for that last little piece to fix a mistake!

★ **Do you press your scraps? I don't!** They get pressed when I'm ready to use them. There's no sense in trying to keep them nice and pretty until then.

★ **My rule of thumb for keeping scraps:** I only keep sizes I know I will use. If a scrap doesn't seem reasonable enough for a common cut size I'd use in the future, then there's no sense in keeping it.

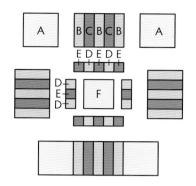

Using B/C/B/C/B, make a strip set; crosscut into 4 segments, 2¼" × 3". Using E/D/E/D/E, make a strip set; crosscut into 2 segments, 1" × 3". Using D/E/D, make a strip set; crosscut into 2 segments, 1" × 2".

Light
A: 4 ☐ 2¼" × 2¼"
F: 1 ☐ 2" × 2"

Medium
B: 3 ▭ 1" × 10"
D: 4 ▭ 1" × 6"

Dark
C: 2 ▭ 1" × 10"
E: 4 ▭ 1" × 6"

✷ **Binding isn't my favorite part of the quilt process.** To make sure quilts don't languish with no binding, I keep a stack of them by my "stitching nest" and have a TV binge-watching marathon to get through a couple at a time.

✷ **I buy charm packs** to get a good idea of what prints I might want to go back and buy yardage of. They're the perfect size to see what the full print actually looks like.

✷ **When I see fabric I like but don't have a specific plan for,** I buy 1/2 yard. It gives enough yardage to make my own curated bundle of either Layer Cakes, Jelly Rolls, charm packs, or Honey Buns.

44 Winter Panes

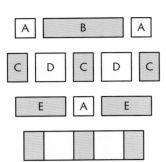

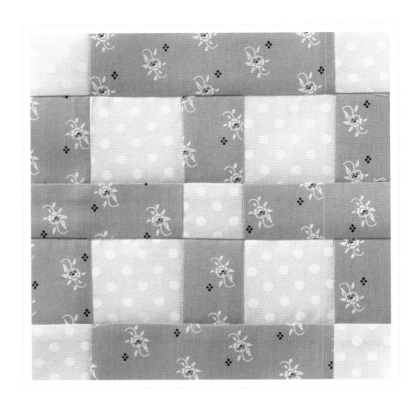

Light
A: 5 ☐ 1½" × 1½"
D: 4 ☐ 2" × 2"

Dark
B: 2 ▭ 1½" × 4½"
C: 6 ▭ 1½" × 2"
E: 2 ▭ 1½" × 3"

45 Courthouse Steps

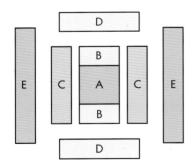

Darks
A: 1 ☐ 2½" × 2½"
C: 2 ▭ 1½" × 4½"
E: 2 ▭ 1½" × 6½"

Light
B: 2 ▭ 1½" × 2½"
D: 2 ▭ 1½" × 4½"

46 Sail Boat

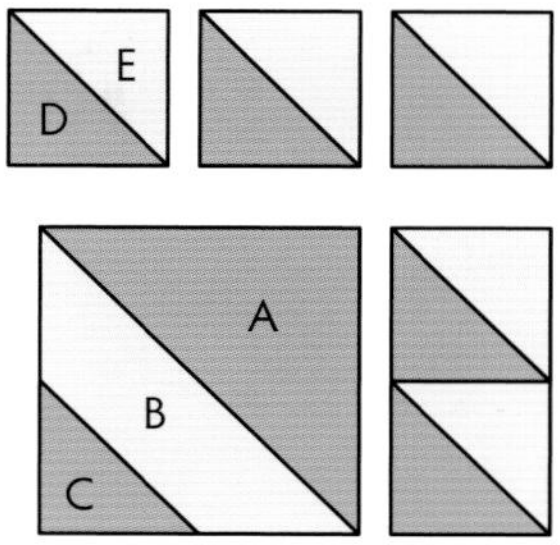

Using A/B, make 4½" HST units (page 6; 1 unit is extra). Using C, make a stitch-and-flip corner (page 7). Using D/E, make 2½" HST units (1 unit is extra).

Dark	Light
A: 1 ☐ 4⅞" × 4⅞"	**B:** 1 ☐ 4⅞" × 4⅞"
C: 1 ☐ 2½" × 2½"	**E:** 3 ☐ 2⅞" × 2⅞"
D: 3 ☐ 2⅞" × 2⅞"	

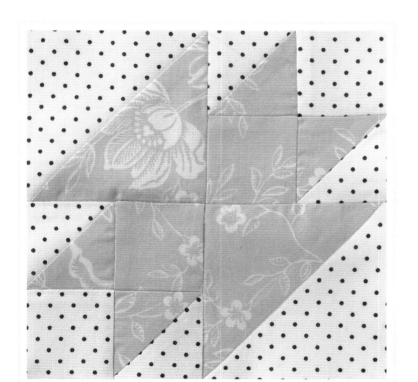

47 Anvil

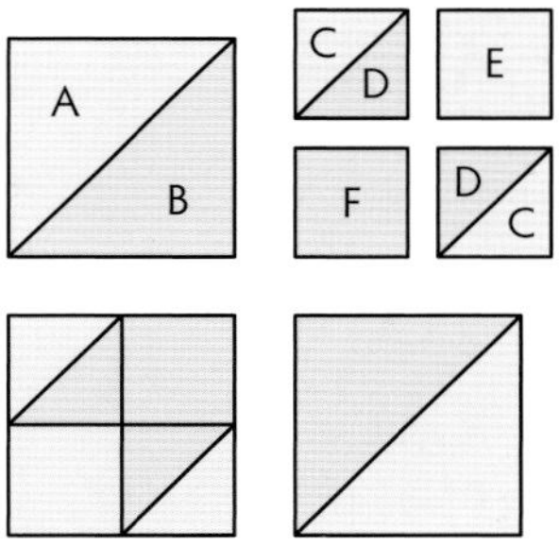

Using A/B, make 3½" HST units (page 6). Using C/D, make 2" HST units.

Light	Medium
A: 1 ☐ 3⅞" × 3⅞"	**B:** 1 ☐ 3⅞" × 3⅞"
C: 2 ☐ 2⅜" × 2⅜"	**D:** 2 ☐ 2⅜" × 2⅜"
E: 2 ☐ 2" × 2"	**F:** 2 ☐ 2" × 2"

48 *Dutch Windmill*

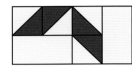

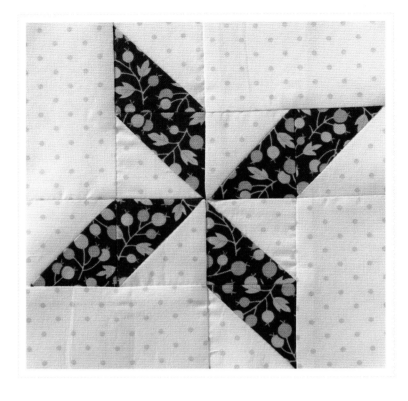

Using A/B, make 2" HST units (page 6).

Light
A: 4 ☐ 2⅜" × 2⅜"
C: 4 ▭ 2" × 3½"

Dark
B: 4 ☐ 2⅜" × 2⅜"

49 *Opposites*

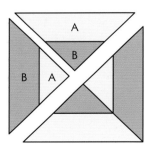

Using A/B, make 2 strip sets. Using the pattern on page 78, make a template (page 7) and cut 2 units with light tips and 2 with dark tips. (See "Rulers" on page 7 to cut the units using a ruler.)

Light
A: 2 ▭ 2" × 12"

Dark
B: 2 ▭ 2" × 12"

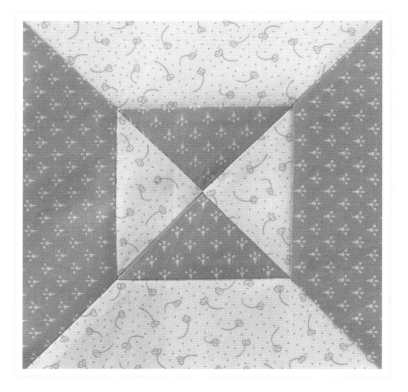

50 Apple Pie

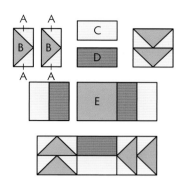

Using A/B, make 1½" × 2½" flying-geese units (page 6).

Light
A: 16 □ 1½" × 1½"
C: 4 ▭ 1½" × 2½"

Dark
D: 4 ▭ 1½" × 2½"

Medium
B: 8 ▭ 1½" × 2½"
E: 1 □ 2½" × 2½"

51 Whirligig

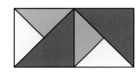

Light
A: 1 ⊠ 4¼" × 4¼"

Medium
B: 1 ⊠ 4¼" × 4¼"

Dark
C: 2 ◫ 3⅞" × 3⅞"

52 Wheels

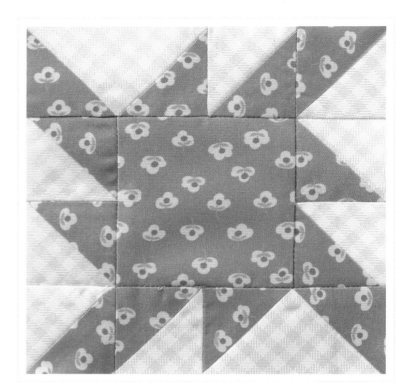

Using A/B, make 2" × 3½" flying-geese units (page 6). Using C/D, make 2" HST units (page 6).

Light
A: 2 ▭ 2" × 3½"
C: 4 ◻ 2⅜" × 2⅜"

Dark
B: 4 ◻ 2" × 2"
D: 4 ◻ 2⅜" × 2⅜"
E: 1 ◻ 3½" × 3½"

53 Cheyenne

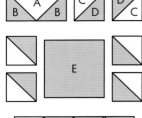

Using A/B, make 2" HST units (page 6). Using C/D, make 2" × 3½" flying-geese units (page 6). Using D/E, make stitch-and-flip corners (page 7).

Light
A: 2 ◻ 2⅜" × 2⅜"

Darks
B: 2 ◻ 2⅜" × 2⅜"
C: 4 ▭ 2" × 3½"
D: 12 ◻ 2" × 2"
E: 1 ◻ 3½" × 3½"

54 All Roads Point to Home

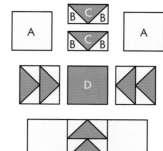

Using B/C, make 1½" × 2½" flying-geese units (page 6).

Light
A: 4 ☐ 2½" × 2½"
B: 16 ☐ 1½" × 1½"

Dark
C: 8 ☐ 1½" × 2½"
D: 1 ☐ 2½" × 2½"

55 Good Vibrations

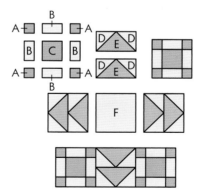

Using D/E, make 1½" × 2½" flying-geese units (page 6).

Dark
A: 16 ☐ 1" × 1"
C: 4 ☐ 1½" × 1½"

Medium
E: 8 ☐ 1½" × 2½"

Light
B: 16 ☐ 1" × 1½"
D: 16 ☐ 1½" × 1½"
F: 1 ☐ 2½" × 2½"

56 Maze

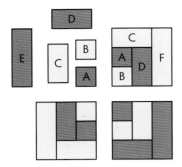

Dark
A: 4 ☐ 1½" × 1½"
D: 4 ▭ 1½" × 2½"
E: 2 ▭ 1½" × 3½"

Light
B: 4 ☐ 1½" × 1½"
C: 4 ▭ 1½" × 2½"
F: 2 ▭ 1½" × 3½"

57 Checkers

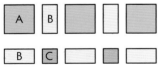

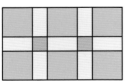

Medium
A: 9 ☐ 2" × 2"

Light
B: 12 ▭ 1¼" × 2"

Dark
C: 4 ☐ 1¼" × 1¼"

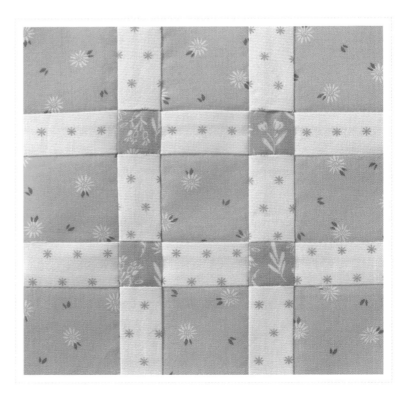

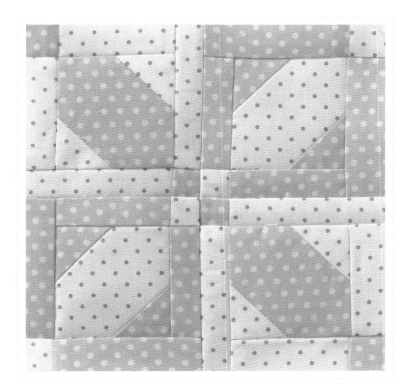

58 Here and There

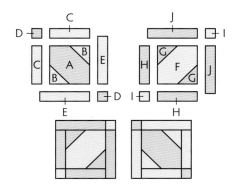

Using B and G, make stitch-and-flip corners (page 7).

Medium
A: 2 ☐ 2½" × 2½"
D: 4 ☐ 1" × 1"
G: 4 ☐ 1½" × 1½"
H: 4 ☐ 1" × 2½"
J: 4 ☐ 1" × 3"

Light
B: 4 ☐ 1½" × 1½"
C: 4 ☐ 1" × 2½"
E: 4 ☐ 1" × 3"
F: 2 ☐ 2½" × 2½"
I: 4 ☐ 1" × 1"

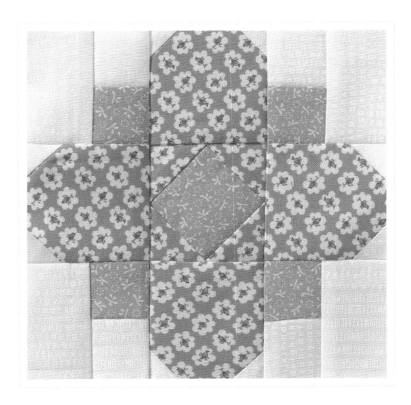

59 Arbor Way

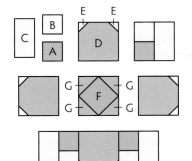

Using E and G, make stitch-and-flip corners (page 7).

Dark
A: 4 ☐ 1½" × 1½"
F: 1 ☐ 2½" × 2½"

Medium
D: 4 ☐ 2½" × 2½"
G: 4 ☐ 1½" × 1½"

Light
B: 4 ☐ 1½" × 1½"
C: 4 ☐ 1½" × 2½"
E: 8 ☐ 1" × 1"

60 Market Square

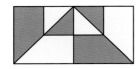

Using A/B, make a strip set. Using the pattern on page 79, make a template (page 7) and cut 4 units with dark tips and 4 with light tips. (See "Rulers" on page 7 to cut the units using a ruler.)

Light
A: 1 ▭ 2" × 17"

Dark
B: 2 ▭ 2" × 17"

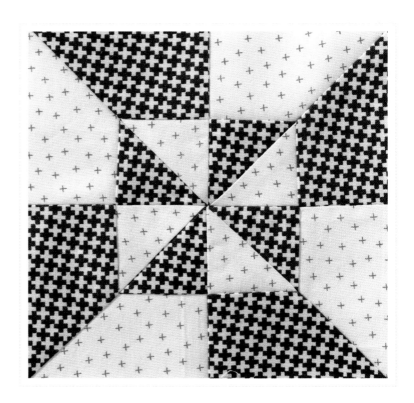

61 Maple Star

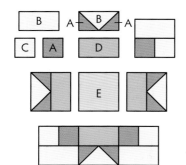

Using A/B, make 1½" × 2½" flying-geese units (page 6).

Darks
A: 12 ▢ 1½" × 1½"

Medium
D: 4 ▭ 1½" × 2½"

Lights
B: 8 ▭ 1½" × 2½"
C: 4 ▢ 1½" × 1½"
E: 1 ▢ 2½" × 2½"

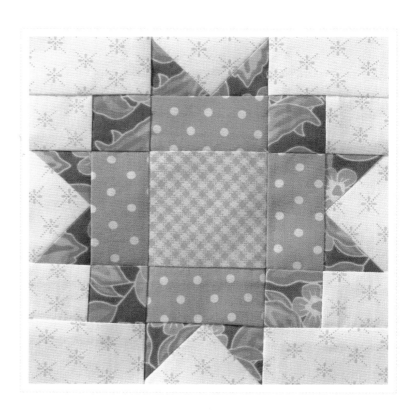

62 Far West

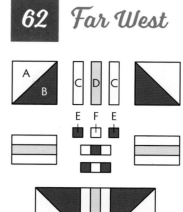

Using A/B, make 2¾" HST units (page 6).

Light
A: 2 ☐ 3⅛" × 3⅛"
C: 8 ▭ 1" × 2¾"
F: 4 ☐ 1" × 1"

Dark
B: 2 ☐ 3⅛" × 3⅛"
E: 5 ☐ 1" × 1"

Medium
D: 4 ▭ 1" × 2¾"

Susan's Scrappy Secrets

⁎ **While I generally buy a half-yard of a fabric** I like, my exception is for ginghams, stripes, and large-scale prints. Checks and stripes make the cutest bias bindings, so I usually buy 1 1/2 yards of the ones I like.

⁎ **To make the best use of fabric and avoid seams,** I like to cut borders on the lengthwise grain. Then I use the remaining long skinny piece to cut the binding and piece whatever's left into the quilt backing.

⁎ **Do you love large-scale prints for quilt borders?** When I use these, I like to fussy cut the leftovers for a matching pillow. Large floral prints and pillows make such a bold statement that you can easily change the look and mood of a room in an instant.

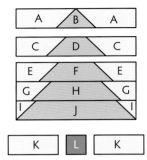

63 Tree

Using A–H, make rectangle-to-rectangle units (page 7). Using I, make stitch-and-flip corners (page 7).

Light
A: 2 ▭ 1½" × 3½"
C: 2 ▭ 1½" × 3"
E: 2 ▭ 1½" × 2⅝"
G: 2 ▭ 1½" × 2¼"
I: 2 ▢ 1½" × 1½"
K: 2 ▭ 1½" × 3"

Medium
B: 1 ▭ 1½" × 2½"
D: 1 ▭ 1½" × 3½"
F: 1 ▭ 1½" × 4¼"
H: 1 ▭ 1½" × 5"
J: 1 ▭ 1½" × 6½"

Dark
L: 1 ▢ 1½" × 1½"

Susan's Scrappy Secrets

* **When fabric shopping, I always hit the sale area first.** Not just for the bargains but also for the smaller yardage on the ends of bolts. These are priced to sell, and I'm sure I can find some pieces I'll love in a future quilt.

* **Have a group of fabrics you want to use,** but feel like you need an additional piece or two to make the perfect combination? Take a picture of the group with your phone so you'll have it handy the next time you're at the quilt shop!

64 Americana

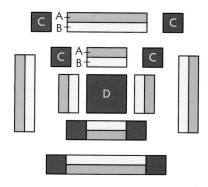

Using A/B, make a strip set; crosscut into 4 segments, 1½" × 4½", and 4 segments, 1½" × 2½".

Medium
A: 1 ☐ 1" × 30"

Light
B: 1 ☐ 1" × 30"

Dark
C: 8 ☐ 1½" × 1½"
D: 1 ☐ 2½" × 2½"

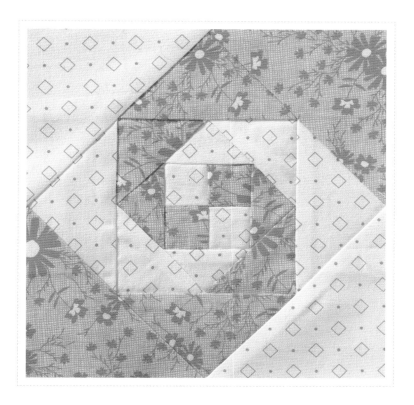

65 Snail's Trail

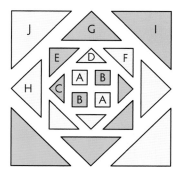

Light
A: 2 ☐ 1¼" × 1¼"
D: 1 ☒ 2¾" × 2¾"
   (2 triangles are extra)
F: 1 ☑ 2⅜" × 2⅜"
H: 1 ☑ 3" × 3"
J: 1 ☑ 3⅞" × 3⅞"

Dark
B: 2 ☐ 1¼" × 1¼"
C: 1 ☒ 2¾" × 2¾"
   (2 triangles are extra)
E: 1 ☑ 2⅜" × 2⅜"
G: 1 ☑ 3" × 3"
I: 1 ☑ 3⅞" × 3⅞"

66 King's Crown

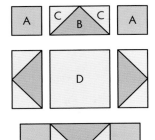

Using B/C, make 2" × 3½" flying-geese units (page 6).

Dark 1
A: 4 ☐ 2" × 2"

Dark 2
B: 4 ▭ 2" × 3½"

Light
C: 8 ☐ 2" × 2"
D: 1 ☐ 3½" × 3½"

67 Jack-in-the-Box

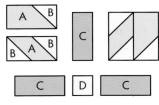

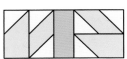

Using B, make stitch-and-flip corners (page 7).

Dark 1
A: 8 ▭ 1¾" × 3"

Dark 2
C: 4 ▭ 1½" × 3"

Light
B: 12 ☐ 1¾" × 1¾"
D: 1 ☐ 1½" × 1½"

68 Mixed Nine Patch

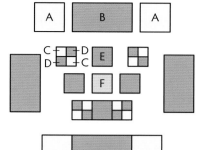

Light
A: 4 □ 2" × 2"
C: 8 □ 1" × 1"

Dark
B: 4 ▭ 2" × 3½"
D: 8 □ 1" × 1"
E: 4 □ 1½" × 1½"

Medium
F: 1 □ 1½" × 1½"

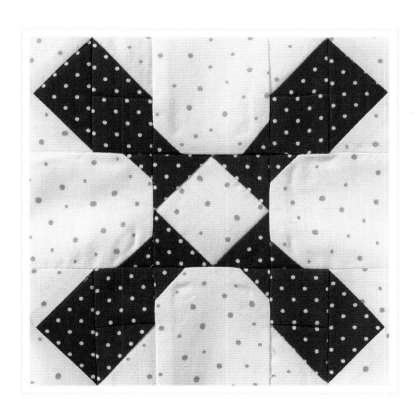

69 Goblets

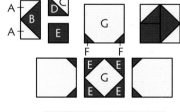

Using A/B, make 1½" × 2½" flying-geese units (page 6). Using C/D, make 1½" HST units (page 6). Using E and F, make stitch-and-flip corners (page 7).

Light
A: 8 □ 1½" × 1½"
C: 2 □ 1⅞" × 1⅞"
G: 5 □ 2½" × 2½"

Dark
B: 4 ▭ 1½" × 2½"
D: 2 □ 1⅞" × 1⅞"
E: 8 □ 1½" × 1½"
F: 8 □ 1" × 1"

70 Spinning Tops

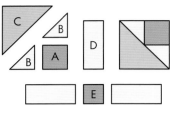
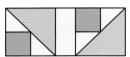
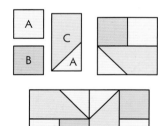

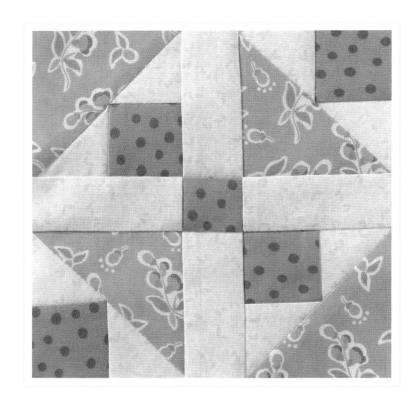

Dark
A: 4 ☐ 1¾" × 1¾"
E: 1 ☐ 1½" × 1½"

Medium
C: 2 ☒ 3⅜" × 3⅜"

Light
B: 4 ☒ 2⅛" × 2⅛"
D: 4 ☐ 1½" × 3"

71 Oh Susannah

Using A, make stitch-and-flip corners (page 7).

Light
A: 8 ☐ 2" × 2"

Dark
B: 4 ☐ 2" × 2"

Medium
C: 4 ☐ 2" × 3½"

72 Four Patch Star

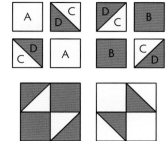

Using C/D, make 2" HST units (page 6).

Light
A: 4 ☐ 2" × 2"
C: 4 ☐ 2⅜" × 2⅜"

Dark
B: 4 ☐ 2" × 2"
D: 4 ☐ 2⅜" × 2⅜"

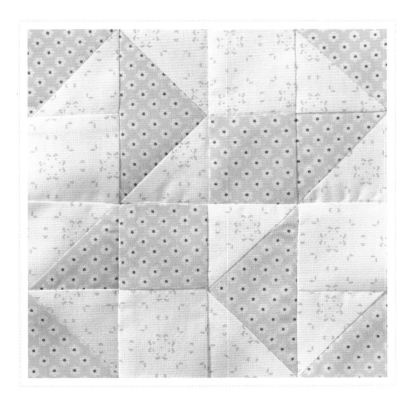

73 New Neighbor

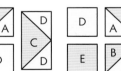
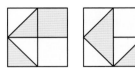

Using A/B, make 2" HST units (page 6).
Using C/D, make 2" × 3½" flying-geese units (page 6).

Light
A: 3 ☐ 2⅜" × 2⅜"
D: 8 ☐ 2" × 2"

Medium
B: 3 ☐ 2⅜" × 2⅜"
C: 2 ▭ 2" × 3½"
E: 2 ☐ 2" × 2"

74 Nine Patch Star

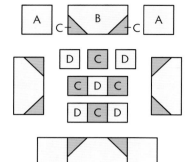

Using C, make stitch-and-flip corners
(page 7).

Light
A: 4 □ 2" × 2"
B: 4 ▭ 2" × 3½"
D: 5 □ 1½" × 1½"

Dark
C: 12 □ 1½" × 1½"

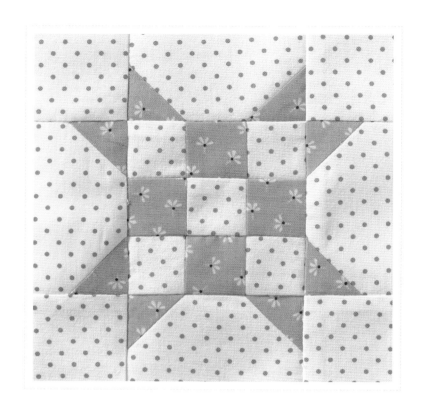

75 The Broken Path

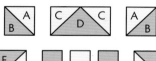
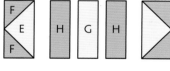

Using A/B, make 2" HST units (page 6).
Using C/D and E/F, make 2" × 3½"
flying-geese units (page 6).

Light
A: 2 □ 2⅜" × 2⅜"
C: 4 □ 2" × 2"
E: 2 ▭ 2" × 3½"
G: 1 ▭ 1½" × 3½"

Dark
B: 2 □ 2⅜" × 2⅜"
D: 2 ▭ 2" × 3½"
F: 4 □ 2" × 2"
H: 2 ▭ 1½" × 3½"

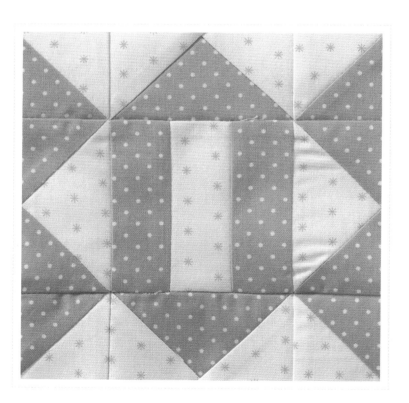

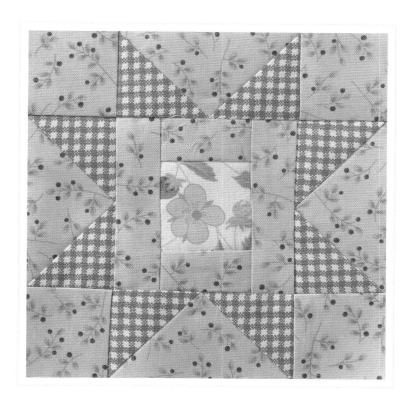

76 Premium Prize

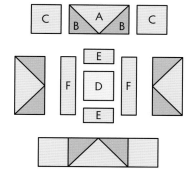

Using A/B, make 2" × 3½" flying-geese units (page 6).

Medium
A: 4 ☐ 2" × 3½"
C: 4 ☐ 2" × 2"
E: 2 ☐ 1¼" × 2"
F: 2 ☐ 1¼" × 3½"

Dark
B: 8 ☐ 2" × 2"

Light
D: 1 ☐ 2" × 2"

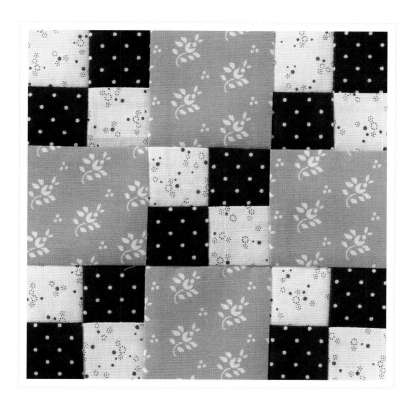

77 Thrifty

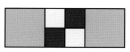

Light
A: 10 ☐ 1½" × 1½"

Dark
B: 10 ☐ 1½" × 1½"

Medium
C: 4 ☐ 2½" × 2½"

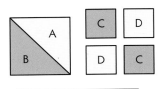

78 The Sickle

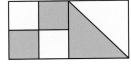

Using A/B, make 3½" HST units (page 6).

Light
A: 1 ☐ 3⅞" × 3⅞"
D: 4 ☐ 2" × 2"

Dark
B: 1 ☐ 3⅞" × 3⅞"
C: 4 ☐ 2" × 2"

79 Double Plain

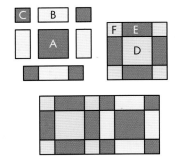

Dark
A: 2 ☐ 2" × 2"
C: 8 ☐ 1¼" × 1¼"
E: 8 ☐ 1¼" × 2"

Light
B: 8 ☐ 1¼" × 2"

Medium
D: 2 ☐ 2" × 2"
F: 8 ☐ 1¼" × 1¼"

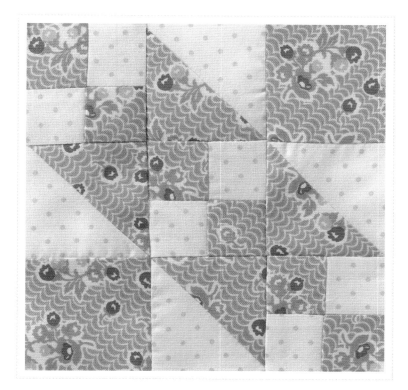

80 Rocky Road to California

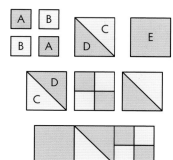

Using C/D, make 2½" HST units (page 6).

Dark
A: 6 ▢ 1½" × 1½"
D: 2 ▢ 2⅞" × 2⅞"
E: 2 ▢ 2½" × 2½"

Light
B: 6 ▢ 1½" × 1½"
C: 2 ▢ 2⅞" × 2⅞"

Susan's Scrappy Secrets

I use the camera in my phone to help out in many ways:

✶ If I'm unsure of my colors in a block, I snap a picture and look at it from all angles. Are the colors in the right places? Do I like them together?

✶ Once a quilt layout is complete, take a picture, then change it to black and white to see if the values are balanced throughout the quilt.

✶ Revert the quilt layout photo back to color to determine if you want to move any blocks around based on the colors and not just values.

✶ When you have a final layout, take a picture and use the rotate function to look at the quilt from four different angles. If it looks good, time to sew the blocks together!

81 Susan's Puzzle

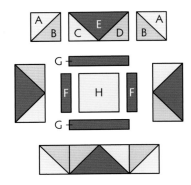

Using A/B, make 2" HST units (page 6).
Using C/D/E, make 2" × 3½" flying-geese units (page 6).

Light
A: 2 ☐ 2⅜" × 2⅜"
C: 4 ☐ 2" × 2"
H: 1 ☐ 2½" × 2½"

Medium
B: 2 ☐ 2⅜" × 2⅜"
D: 4 ☐ 2" × 2"

Dark
E: 4 ▭ 2" × 3½"
F: 2 ▭ 1" × 2½"
G: 2 ▭ 1" × 3½"

Susan's Scrappy Secrets

* **I may be known for making scrappy quilts,** but most of them start as two-color quilts with my first two picks of fabric. My fabric choices grow from there, but I always keep my first two choices in the quilt no matter how many other fabrics I add to the mix.

* **When laying out blocks for a scrappy quilt** (or a sampler quilt like this one), start with the block with colors you're most confident of, and move the block around the quilt.

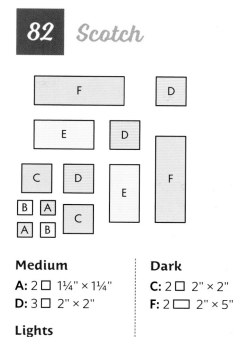

82 Scotch

Medium
A: 2 □ 1¼" × 1¼"
D: 3 □ 2" × 2"

Lights
B: 2 □ 1¼" × 1¼"
E: 2 ▭ 2" × 3½"

Dark
C: 2 □ 2" × 2"
F: 2 ▭ 2" × 5"

★ **Need some fresh color inspiration?** Shop the produce department at your local market. Treat it like a quilt shop and mix and match the colors of fruits and veggies for a fun new way of looking at color combinations.

★ **Speaking of food,** I love pretty packaging on grocery store items and will bring them home, keep the packages, and store the food in a different container. These unexpected sources of color inspiration may be a great jumping off point for your next quilt.

83 *Basket*

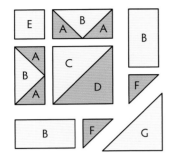

Using A/B, make 2" × 3½" flying-geese units (page 6). Using C/D, make 3½" HST units (page 6; 1 unit is extra).

Dark
A: 4 ☐ 2" × 2"
D: 1 ☐ 3⅞" × 3⅞"
F: 1 ☑ 2⅜" × 2⅜"

Light
B: 4 ☐ 2" × 3½"
C: 1 ☐ 3⅞" × 3⅞"
E: 1 ☐ 2" × 2"
G: 1 ☑ 3⅞" × 3⅞"
   (1 triangle is extra)

Susan's Scrappy Secrets

★ **Continue the cute fabrics from your quilt blocks** all the way to the edge of the quilt by adding a pieced border. Get creative!

★ **Try incorporating scrappy sashing into a scrappy quilt.** Once your blocks are laid out how you like them, you can move the various pieces of sashing around to see if scrappy sashing works and if you like it for that project.

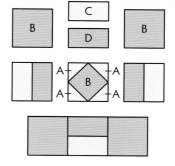

Using A, make stitch-and-flip corners (page 7).

Light
A: 4 ☐ 1½" × 1½"
C: 4 ▭ 1½" × 2½"

Dark
B: 5 ☐ 2½" × 2½"
D: 4 ▭ 1½" × 2½"

★ **I've never met anyone in a quilt shop who doesn't love what they do.** Run to them with all your questions, from techniques to help with color planning. Take your scraps with you if you want some color help. I promise, they'll love helping you. They're a great source of hands-on help.

★ **Don't be afraid to show someone your mistakes.** It's the best way to learn how to do things better the next time.

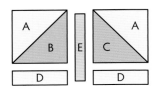

85 *Toy Boat*

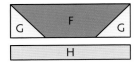

Using A/B and A/C, make 3¼" HST units (page 6; 1 of each unit is extra). Using G, make stitch-and-flip corners (page 7).

Light
A: 2 □ 3⅝" × 3⅝"
D: 2 ▭ 1¼" × 3¼"
G: 2 □ 2¼" × 2¼"

Darks
B: 1 □ 3⅝" × 3⅝"
C: 1 □ 3⅝" × 3⅝"
F: 1 ▭ 2¼" × 6½"

Mediums
E: 1 ▭ 1" × 4"
H: 1 ▭ 1¼" × 6½"

Susan's Scrappy Secrets

✷ **When making a new pattern,** jump to the cutting list—you may not have a ½ yard of pink floral, but maybe you have scraps and strips or fat quarters that are sufficient to cut what you need. So look before you shop!

✷ **If it turns out you don't like the fabric choice** in a particular quilt block, don't fret. It's only a small amount of fabric, so remake it until you're happy. Just chalk it up to a lesson learned and know that you'll love your quilt more because you *didn't* force yourself to use that block.

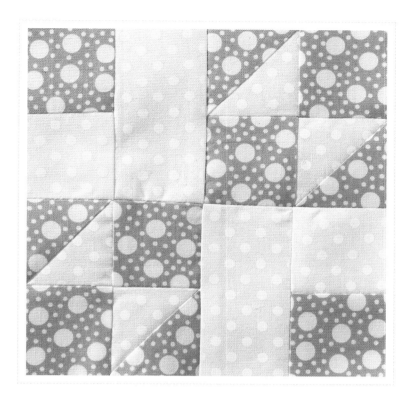

86 Double V

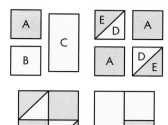

Using D/E, make 2" HST units (page 6).

Dark
A: 6 ☐ 2" × 2"
E: 2 ☐ 2⅜" × 2⅜"

Light
B: 2 ☐ 2" × 2"
C: 2 ▭ 2" × 3½"
D: 2 ☐ 2⅜" × 2⅜"

87 Framed Nine Patch

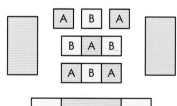

Dark
A: 5 ☐ 1½" × 1½"
D: 4 ▭ 2" × 3½"

Light
B: 4 ☐ 1½" × 1½"
C: 4 ☐ 2" × 2"

88 Forest Paths

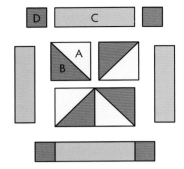

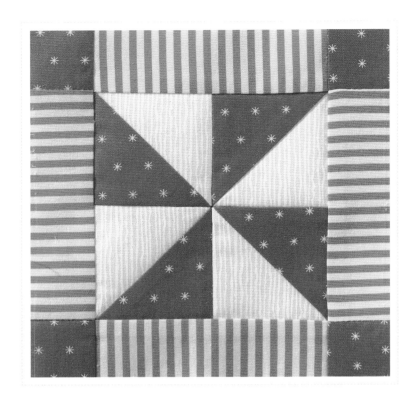

Using A/B, make 2½" HST units (page 6).

Light
A: 2 ☐ 2⅞" × 2⅞"

Medium
C: 4 ▭ 1½" × 4½"

Dark
B: 2 ☐ 2⅞" × 2⅞"
D: 4 ☐ 1½" × 1½"

89 Equinox

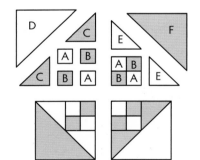

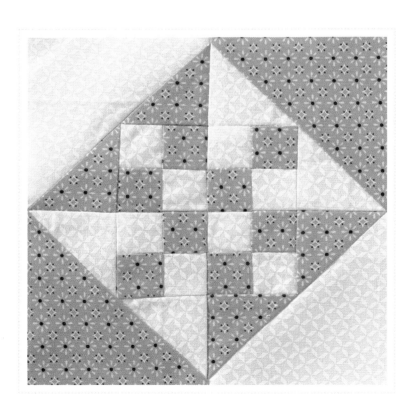

Light
A: 8 ☐ 1¼" × 1¼"
D: 1 ☑ 3⅞" × 3⅞"
E: 2 ☑ 2⅜" × 2⅜"

Dark
B: 8 ☐ 1¼" × 1¼"
C: 2 ☑ 2⅜" × 2⅜"
F: 1 ☑ 3⅞" × 3⅞"

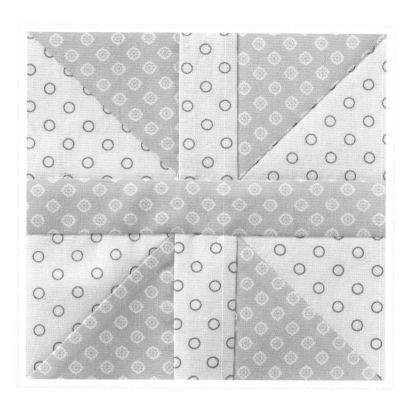

90 Diamond Panes

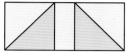

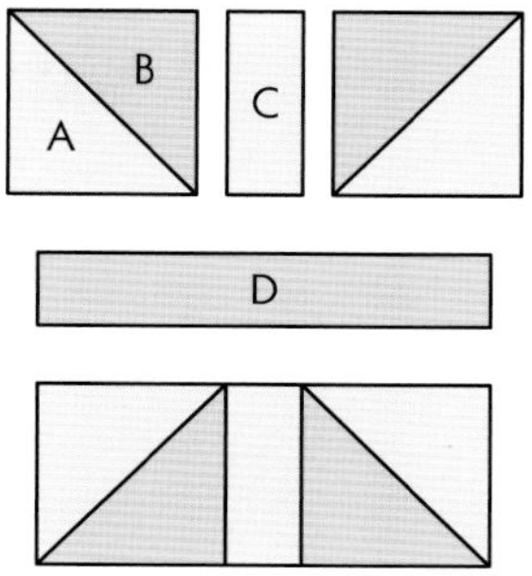

Using A/B, make 3" HST units (page 6).

Light	Dark
A: 2 ☐ 3⅜" × 3⅜"	**B:** 2 ☐ 3⅜" × 3⅜"
C: 2 ▭ 1½" × 3"	**D:** 1 ▭ 1½" × 6½"

91 Grandma Knows Best

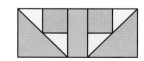

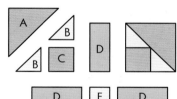

Dark	Light
A: 2 ◩ 3⅜" × 3⅜"	**B:** 4 ◩ 2⅛" × 2⅛"
C: 4 ☐ 1¾" × 1¾"	**E:** 1 ☐ 1½" × 1½"
	Medium
	D: 4 ▭ 1½" × 3"

92 Geese and Goslings

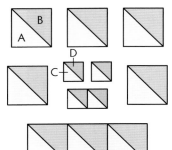

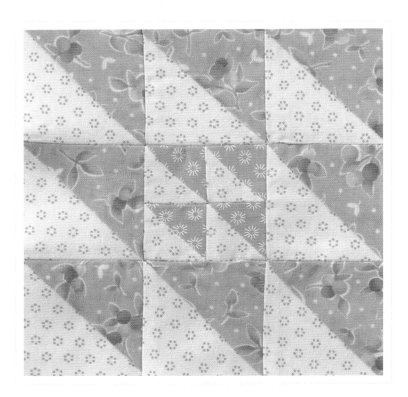

Using A/B, make 2½" HST units (page 6).
Using C/D, make 1½" HST units.

Light
A: 4 ☐ 2⅞" × 2⅞"
C: 2 ☐ 1⅞" × 1⅞"

Darks
B: 4 ☐ 2⅞" × 2⅞"
D: 2 ☐ 1⅞" × 1⅞"

93 Hour Glass

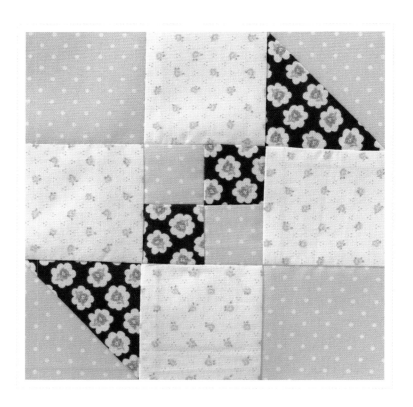

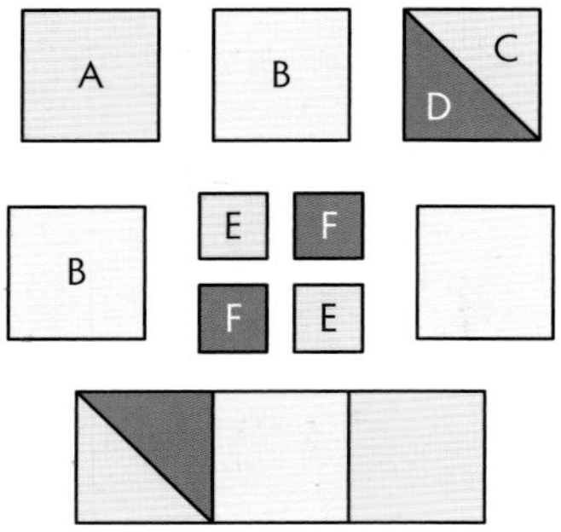

Using C/D, make 2½" HST units (page 6).

Medium
A: 2 ☐ 2½" × 2½"
C: 1 ☐ 2⅞" × 2⅞"
E: 2 ☐ 1½" × 1½"

Light
B: 4 ☐ 2½" × 2½"

Dark
D: 1 ☐ 2⅞" × 2⅞"
F: 2 ☐ 1½" × 1½"

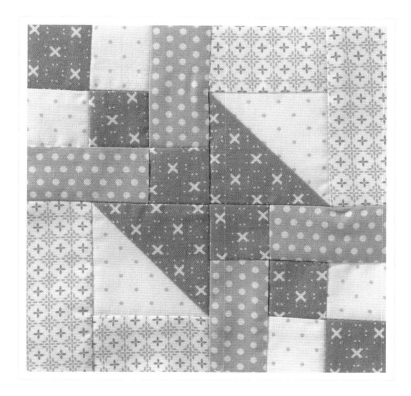

94 Hayes Corner

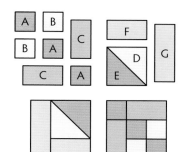

Using D/E, make 2½" HST units (page 6).

Darks
A: 6 ☐ 1½" × 1½"
C: 4 ▭ 1½" × 2½"
E: 1 ☐ 2⅞" × 2⅞"

Light
B: 4 ☐ 1½" × 1½"
D: 1 ☐ 2⅞" × 2⅞"

Medium
F: 2 ▭ 1½" × 2½"
G: 2 ▭ 1½" × 3½"

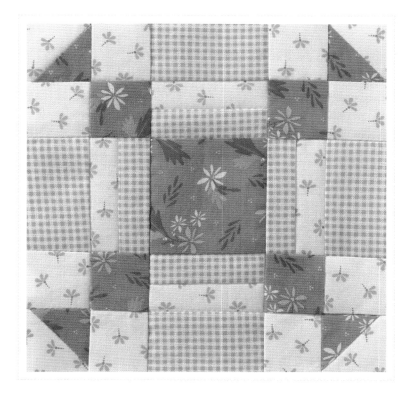

95 Almost Churn Dash

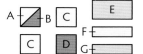

Using A/B, make 1½" HST units (page 6).

Light
A: 2 ☐ 1⅞" × 1⅞"
C: 8 ☐ 1½" × 1½"
F: 4 ▭ 1" × 2½"

Dark
B: 2 ☐ 1⅞" × 1⅞"
D: 4 ☐ 1½" × 1½"
H: 1 ☐ 2½" × 2½"

Medium
E: 4 ▭ 1½" × 2½"
G: 4 ▭ 1" × 2½"

96 *Broken Windows*

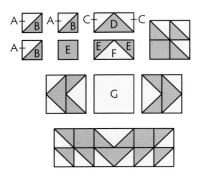

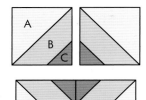

Using A/B, make 1½" HST units (page 6).
Using C/D and E/F, make 1½" × 2½"
flying-geese units (page 6).

Light
A: 6 ☐ 1⅞" × 1⅞"
C: 8 ☐ 1½" × 1½"
F: 4 ☐ 1½" × 2½"
G: 1 ☐ 2½" × 2½"

Dark
B: 6 ☐ 1⅞" × 1⅞"
D: 4 ☐ 1½" × 2½"
E: 12 ☐ 1½" × 1½"

97 *Depression*

Using A/B, make 3½" HST units (page 6).
Using C, make stitch-and-flip corners
(page 7).

Light
A: 2 ☐ 3⅞" × 3⅞"

Medium
B: 2 ☐ 3⅞" × 3⅞"

Dark
C: 4 ☐ 1¾" × 1¾"

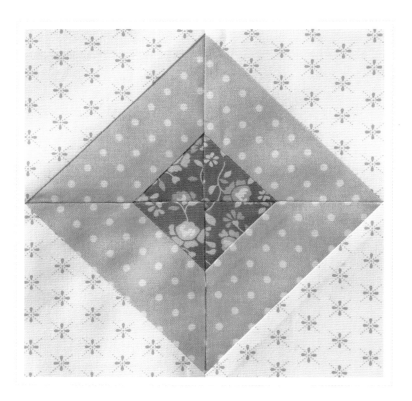

98 Boxed Star

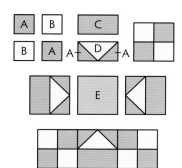

Using A/D, make 1½" × 2½" flying-geese units (page 6).

Dark		Light	
A: 16 □ 1½" × 1½"		**B:** 8 □ 1½" × 1½"	
C: 4 ▭ 1½" × 2½"		**D:** 4 ▭ 1½" × 2½"	

Medium

E: 1 □ 2½" × 2½"

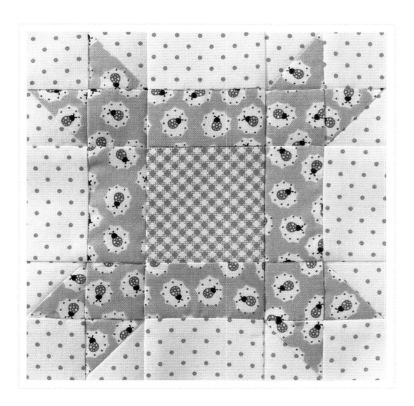

99 Fancy Frame

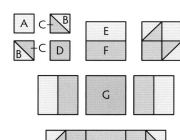

Using B/C, make 1½" HST units (page 6).

Light		Darks	
A: 4 □ 1½" × 1½"		**C:** 4 □ 1⅞" × 1⅞"	
B: 4 □ 1⅞" × 1⅞"		**D:** 4 □ 1½" × 1½"	
E: 4 ▭ 1½" × 2½"		**F:** 4 ▭ 1½" × 2½"	
		G: 1 □ 2½" × 2½"	

100 Hatchet

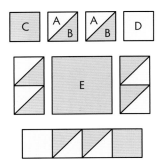

Using A/B, make 2" HST units (page 6).

Light
A: 4 ☐ 2⅜" × 2⅜"
D: 2 ☐ 2" × 2"

Dark
B: 4 ☐ 2⅜" × 2⅜"
C: 2 ☐ 2" × 2"
E: 1 ☐ 3½" × 3½"

101 Framed Ohio Star

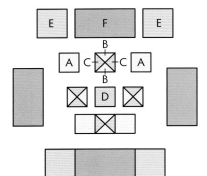

Light
A: 4 ☐ 1½" × 1½"
B: 2 ⊠ 2¼" × 2¼"

Medium
C: 2 ⊠ 2¼" × 2¼"
D: 1 ☐ 1½" × 1½"
E: 4 ☐ 2" × 2"

Dark
F: 4 ▭ 2" × 3½"

102 Boxed In

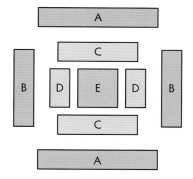

Darks

A: 2 ☐ 1½" × 6½"
B: 2 ☐ 1½" × 4½"
E: 1 ☐ 2½" × 2½"

Light

C: 2 ☐ 1½" × 4½"
D: 2 ☐ 1½" × 2½"

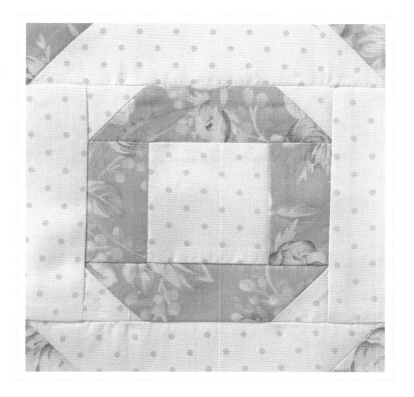

103 Rolling Stone

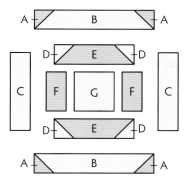

Using A and D, make stitch-and-flip corners (page 7).

Dark

A: 4 ☐ 1½" × 1½"
E: 2 ☐ 1½" × 4½"
F: 2 ☐ 1½" × 2½"

Light

B: 2 ☐ 1½" × 6½"
C: 2 ☐ 1½" × 4½"
D: 4 ☐ 1½" × 1½"
G: 1 ☐ 2½" × 2½"

104 Roman Stripes

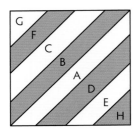

Using A/B, make 6½" HST units (page 6; 1 unit is extra). Using C–H, make stitch-and-flip corners (page 7).

Light	Dark
A: 1 ☐ 6⅞" × 6⅞"	**B:** 1 ☐ 6⅞" × 6⅞"
C: 1 ☐ 5¼" × 5¼"	**D:** 1 ☐ 5¼" × 5¼"
E: 1 ☐ 3¾" × 3¾"	**F:** 1 ☐ 3¾" × 3¾"
G: 1 ☐ 2⅜" × 2⅜"	**H:** 1 ☐ 2⅜" × 2⅜"

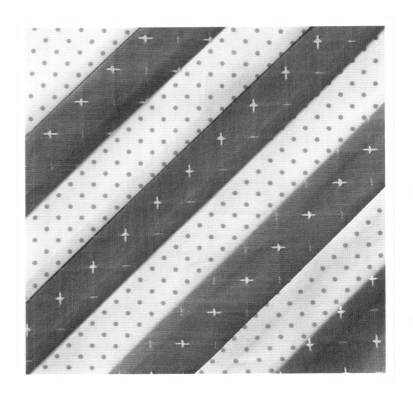

105 New Four Patch

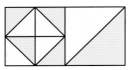

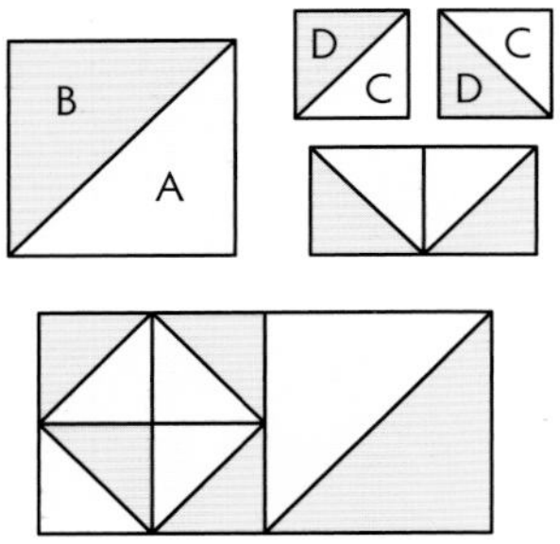

Using A/B, make 3½" HST units (page 6). Using C/D, make 2" HST units.

Light	Medium
A: 1 ☐ 3⅞" × 3⅞"	**B:** 1 ☐ 3⅞" × 3⅞"
C: 4 ☐ 2⅜" × 2⅜"	**D:** 4 ☐ 2⅜" × 2⅜"

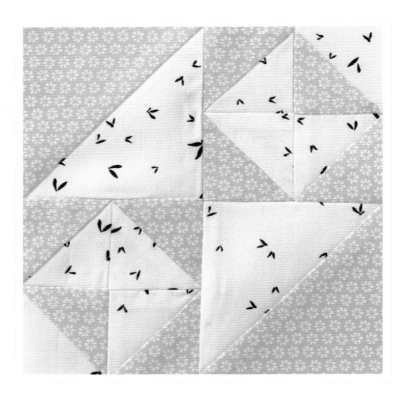

106 Cutting Corners

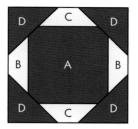

Using D, make stitch-and-flip corners
(page 7).

Dark	Light
A: 1 ☐ 4½" × 4½"	**B:** 2 ☐ 1½" × 4½"
D: 4 ☐ 3" × 3"	**C:** 2 ☐ 1½" × 6½"

Susan's Scrappy Secrets

★ **My go-to storage places for individual quilt projects are**
14" x 14" scrapbook storage boxes. I buy the clear ones so I
can see each project at a glance.

★ **Do you like to join block-of-the-month programs,
stitch-alongs, and such?** They can be so much fun, but
don't ever feel like you're behind. It's your quilt and you
can feel comfortable sewing at your own pace and when
you have time. You're never behind on your own work!

The Templates

PAGE 18

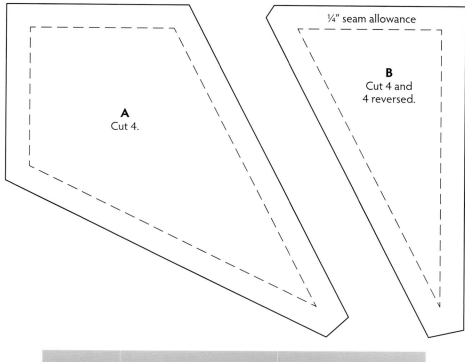

A
Cut 4.

¼" seam allowance

B
Cut 4 and
4 reversed.

Block 09 Tussy Mussy

PAGE 20

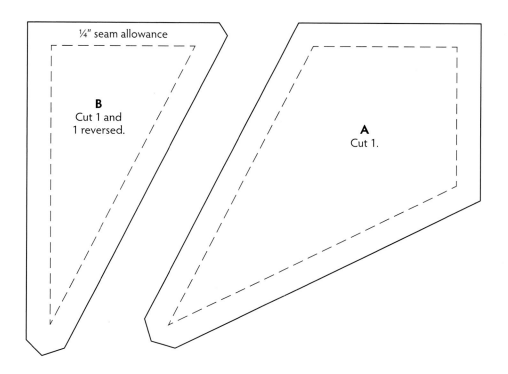

¼" seam allowance

B
Cut 1 and
1 reversed.

A
Cut 1.

PAGE 35

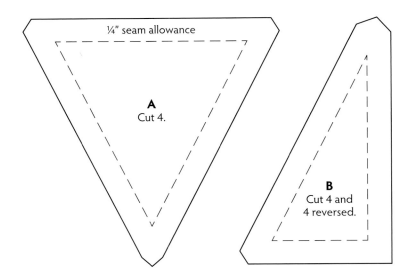

¼" seam allowance

A
Cut 4.

B
Cut 4 and
4 reversed.

PAGE 42

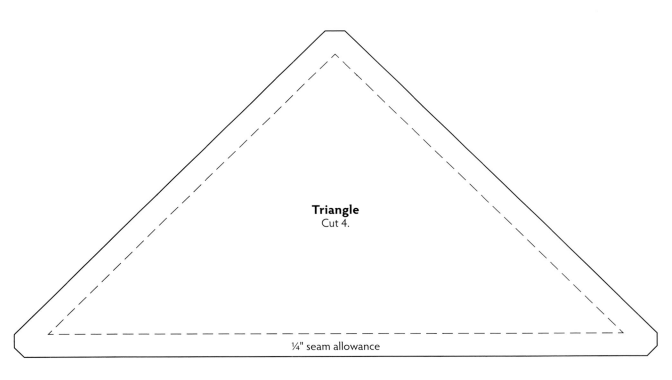

Triangle
Cut 4.

¼" seam allowance

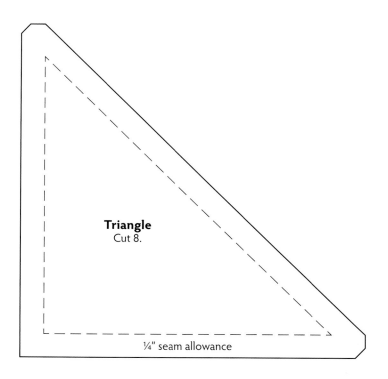

Triangle
Cut 8.

¼" seam allowance

About the Author

Knowing only that she wanted to feature embroidery and Nine Patch blocks, Susan Ache taught herself to make her first quilt. Quiltmaking opened up a new world to this mom of five now-grown children. She turned many hours of reading about quiltmaking into a lifelong passion for creating beautiful quilts.

Susan finds color inspiration in her native Florida surroundings. She's always searching for new and fun ways to show off as many colors as she can in a quilt. Most of her quilts are a creative impulse inspired by a trip to the garden center, a photograph in a magazine, or a few paint-color samples. She never sees just the quilt—she sees the room where the quilt belongs. Working in a quilt store for years helped cultivate Susan's love of color and fabric. Visit Susan on Pinterest and Instagram as @yardgrl60.